AMERICA'S INDUSTRIAL SOCIETY IN THE 19TH CENTURY ™

The Sherman Antitrust Act

Getting Big Business Under Control

Holly Cefrey

rosen central
Primary Source™

The Rosen Publishing Group, Inc., New York

Published in 2004 by The Rosen Publishing Group, Inc.
29 East 21st Street, New York, NY 10010

Copyright © 2004 by The Rosen Publishing Group, Inc.

First Edition

Library of Congress Cataloging-in-Publication Data
Cefrey, Holly.
The Sherman Antitrust Act: getting big business under control/by Holly Cefrey.
     v. cm.—(America's industrial society in the 19th century)
Includes bibliographical references and index.
Contents: Life in the 1800s—Big business—The Sherman Antitrust Act—Protecting American ways.
ISBN 0-8239-4032-2 (library binding)
ISBN 0-8239-4286-4 (paperback)
6-pack ISBN 0-8239-4298-8
1. United States. Sherman Act—Juvenile literature. 2. Antitrust law—United States—History—Juvenile literature. [1. United States—Sherman Act. 2. Antitrust law.]
I. Title. II. Series.

KF1636.525.C44 2003
343.73'0721—dc21
                                                              2002153696

Manufactured in the United States of America

On the cover: large image: Standard Oil Company, Richmond, California. First row (from left to right): steamship docked at a landing; Tammany Hall on election night, 1859; map showing U.S. railroad routes in 1883; detail of banknote, 1822, Bank of the Commonwealth of Kentucky; People's Party (Populist) Convention at Columbus, Nebraska, 1890; Republican ticket, 1865. Second row (from left to right): William McKinley gives a campaign speech in 1896; parade banner of the Veterans of the Haymarket Riot; Alexander Graham Bell's sketch of the telephone, c. 1876; public declaration of the government's ability to crush monopolies; city planners' illustration of Stockton, California; railroad construction camp, Nebraska, 1889.

Photo credits: cover, pp. 11, 20 © Library of Congress; pp. 5, 15 © Library of Congress Prints and Photographs Division; p. 8 courtesy of *New York in the Nineteenth Century,* Dover Publications; p. 9 © Record Group 11, General Records of the U.S. Government/Old Military and Civil Records, National Archives and Records Administration; p. 13 © Bettmann/Corbis; p. 21 courtesy of the National Archives and Records Administration; p. 25 © Michael Nicholson/Corbis; p. 26 © *Chicago Daily News* Negatives Collection, Chicago Historical Society.

Designer: Tahara Hasan; **Editor:** Mark Beyer

Contents

The Need for National Laws

The Sherman Antitrust Act is an important part of American history. It was the first act that controlled big business. Big business ran the largest companies in the nation. The federal government wanted to pass laws to protect smaller businesses. Some of these companies did business nationwide. Others did business only within a single state. The federal government wanted to protect all businesses. Therefore, it had to pass a national act. The Sherman Antitrust Act helped the government control big companies all over the United States.

Big businesses can be so powerful that they put other companies out of business. These large companies have the power to raise or lower the prices for entire markets. Examples of markets include computers, music, and

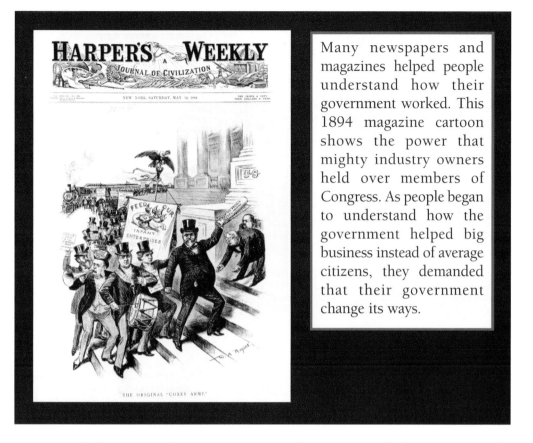

Many newspapers and magazines helped people understand how their government worked. This 1894 magazine cartoon shows the power that mighty industry owners held over members of Congress. As people began to understand how the government helped big business instead of average citizens, they demanded that their government change its ways.

automobiles. Big business can also control the materials that are needed to make products or goods.

These are not necessarily good things. When big business uses its power in these ways, fair competition cannot happen. Fair competition exists when any company has a chance to succeed. This allows even small businesses to succeed. It means that big business cannot do anything to stop small businesses from succeeding.

Fair competition between companies often leads to new inventions. Companies compete against each other to provide the best goods and services. Companies invent ways to make products better. They invent ways to provide better services. They also invent new products and services.

Fair competition also allows the consumer to choose between many businesses when buying goods or services. The consumer is you, your friends, your parents, and everyone you know. The consumer buys and uses goods and services from companies. Most consumers want to buy the best goods and services for the least amount of money. Companies compete against each other to get the most consumers.

Some big companies may try to join together to control a market. They form a trust. A trust is when big companies join together to abuse power. The companies work together to get rid of competition. They work together to control the prices of products or services. The Sherman Antitrust Act was the first set of laws to make trusts illegal. The act stops trusts from happening. This is what is meant by the word "antitrust." It means "against trusts." The Sherman Antitrust Act is still used today. It is used to protect fair competition between businesses.

2
Life in the 1800s

The Sherman Antitrust Act was passed in 1890. Congress made the law to control business in America. It was made after years of public protest. The public was against the abuse of power by big business. Big business abused power because the nation's population was growing fast. More and more consumers crowded into American cities and towns each year. Many businesses made huge fortunes by selling goods and services to these consumers.

The American people won independence from England in 1783. A new government was made for the new nation. The outline for the new government was given in the Constitution of the United States. The Constitution also briefly included another important issue. The issue was business.

America was a land of great promise for business. It had many resources. The resources included lumber, furs, land,

Immigrants arriving from Europe in the 1800s were eager to get jobs. They wanted to start a new life in a new country. Factories took advantage of such workers. Immigrants were paid little money and worked in unsafe conditions. They did not dare to complain because dozens of other immigrants were waiting to take their jobs.

coal, and gold. Fortunes were built from the trade and sale of such resources. People became rich overnight. Millions of immigrants from Europe came to America. They wanted to take part in the land of riches.

The Constitution gave Congress the right to regulate or control trade and business. Congress could control

business deals that took place between the states and with foreign nations. This meant that Congress could make laws that businesses had to follow. This was a tricky thing to do. Successful businesses brought money into a state and helped build a stronger nation. Congress had to be careful about the laws that it made about business. Congress did not want to pass laws that would make businesses fail.

Many early American businesses were farms and livestock ranches. Up until 1870, only 25 percent of

The Constitution of the United States determined which levels of the government controlled commerce throughout the country. Laws were passed to help business grow. Small businesses had to be protected from the power of big businesses.

Americans lived in cities. Everyone else was ranching, farming, mining, or taming wild western lands.

During the early 1800s, most businesses were local or small. Businesses that made goods usually had a few workers. The workers made the goods by hand. Making things by hand meant that it took a long time to make goods. Many businesses also lacked the money to grow larger or improve.

The nation grew quickly during and after the Civil War. This was a war between the Northern and Southern states. It lasted from 1861 to 1865. Factories were built to supply troops with needed goods such as boots and guns. Machines were used to make the goods quickly.

Investors and bankers saw how machines made goods quickly. This meant that more goods could be sold to many open markets. Investors and bankers loaned money to small businesses that wanted to grow. This allowed business owners to buy machines for their factories. Soon many factories were using machines to make goods.

The Kentucky Farmer published news about the agriculture business. Farmers began to form business groups in the mid-1800s to help market and sell produce. Railroad shipping companies often took advantage of farmers. They charged high delivery rates and paid little for the produce.

THE KENTUCKY FARMER.

Vol. I.   VERSAILLES, KY. JUNE 19, 1824.   No. 1.

PRINTED AND PUBLISHED BY
E. G. M'GINNIS & S. RAILEY

At *one dollar twenty five cents, specie.* in advance; or *one dollar seventy-five cents* at the end of the year.

If paid within three months after subscribing it will be considered in advance.

Subscriptions will be continued until all arrearages are paid, unless at the discretion of the Editors—and a failure to notify a discontinuance at the expiration of the time subscribed for, will be considered as a new engagement.

THE FARMER.

In presenting our subscribers with the first number of the KENTUCKY FARMER, and soliciting a more extensive patronage, we are aware of the difficulties with which we have to contend. The number of papers already published in this country, and its pecuniary embarrassments, we believe are among the most prominent. The *first*, would, entirely, have superseded our undertaking, had *any*, or a sufficient number of them been devoted to the farming interest. While they amuse their readers with the idea of their being *checks* and *balances* to the constitution, they neglect to check the progress of indolence and *extravagance* by encouraging a *balance* of *industry*; without which, Kentucky must soon become more fallen and degraded than she is. To awake, so far as practicable, the sleeping energies of her citizens, and to invite them to the investigation of a subject, in which they are more than any other interested, we have established in one of the finest counties, and near the centre of the state, a vehicle for the transmission of farming intelligence. The increase of its utility and importance, will depend upon the encouragement her citizens think proper to give it. But if they patronize *twenty-six* papers on politics by which their condition *may be* improved; we think they will not fail to encourage *one* on *agriculture*, by which their existence *must* be supported. Whilst we confidently hope to elicit the talents of our own citizens on this subject, we believe that if their false delicacy should produce an entire failure in this part of our plan, our access to existing publications, such as the "American Farmer," the "Plough Boy," &c. will enable us to present them with a compilation worth many times more than their subscription.

This paper contains eight pages, printed in such form as to admit of being bound. In the year it will contain four hundred and sixteen pages, of matter, in which every class is interested. The mercury in the Thermometer is not more affected by the state of the atmosphere, than is every other profession, by the advancement or deterioration of the Farmer.

Agricultural,

Awake! my pen, awake my soul!
Survey the globe from pole to pole.
To what employment shall I bow,
Pursue the Arts or hold the Plough?
Upon a just and strict attention,
The Plough appears a high invention.
The great Messiah, when he wrought,
Made ploughs & yokes, as we are taught,
Mogul, renown'd in India's land,
First takes the plough into his hand;
His millions then in honor toil,
To pulverize the fertile soil.
The immortal Job, more rich and grand
Than any in the eastern land.
Launched his plough, the earth gave way,
His thousand oxen rend the clay.
If then the plough supports the nation,
Men of rank and every station,
Let kings to *Farmers* make a bow,
And every man procure a plough.

FROM THE ARATOR.

The present state of Agriculture.

A patient must know that he is sick, before he will take physick. A collection of a few facts, to ascertain the ill health of Agriculture, is necessary to invigorate our efforts towards a cure. One, apparent to the most superficial observer, is, that our land has diminished in fertility. Arts improve the work of nature. When they injure it, they are not arts, but barbarous customs. It is the office of Agriculture as an art, not to impoverish, but to fertilize the soil, and make it more useful than in its natural state. Such is the effect of every species of Agriculture, which can aspire to the character of an art—Its object being to furnish man with articles of the first necessity; whatever defeats that object, is a crime of the first magnitude. Had men the power to obscure or brighten the light of the sun, by obscuring it, they would imitate the morality of diminishing the fertility of the earth,—

is not one as criminal as the other? Yet it is a fact, that lands in their natural state are more valuable, than those which have undergone our habit of Agriculture, of which emigrations are complete proofs.

The decay of a multitude of small towns, so situated as to depend for support on unalterable districts, is another proof of the impoverishment of the soil. It is true that a few large towns have grown up, but this is owing, not to an increased product, but to an increased pasture; whereas, in every case, where the pasture is limited, or isolated by local circumstances, small towns have sprung up, whilst the lands were fresh, and decayed as they were worn out. I have no facts to ascertain certainly the products of Agriculture at different periods relatively to the number of people; such would furnish a demonstration of its state. But I have understood that sixty thousand hogsheads of tobacco, were exported from Virginia, when it contained about one fourth of its present population. If so, had the fertility of the country remained undiminished, Virginia ought now to export two hundred and forty thousand hogsheads, or an equivalent. In this estimate, every species of export except tobacco, is excluded at one epoch, and exports of every other kind included at the other; yet the latter would fall far short of exibiting the equivalent necessary to bring itself on a footing, as to Agriculture, with the former. Two hundred and forty thousand hogsheads of tobacco, which, or an equivalent, Virginia would now export, if the state of Agriculture had been as flourishing as it was sixty or seventy years past, at the present value, by which all our exports are rated, would be worth above seventeen millions of dollars; and supposing Virginia to furnish one seventh part of the native Agricultural exports of the United States, these ought now to amount to one hundred and twenty millions of dollars, had the products kept pace with the increase of population. If this statement is not exactly correct, enough of it certainly is so, to demonstrate a rapid impoverishment of the soil of the United States.

The decay of the culture of tobacco is testimony to this unwelcome fact. It is deserted because the lands are exhausted. To conceal from ourselves a disagreeable truth, we resort to the delusion, that tobacco requires new or fresh land; whereas ev-

Railroads were built across America during the mid-1800s. This allowed goods to be shipped quickly to almost anywhere in America. People also used railroads for travel because it was safer and quicker than travel by horse or wagon. Companies that owned railroads became powerful. Railroad owners became millionaires.

Time of Invention

Toward the end of the 1800s, many factories were built. These factories made new inventions for eager consumers. Many factories used machines to make the goods. This meant that many goods could be made quickly. These factories are known as industrial factories. Factories were built in many cities. The cities became crowded with people wanting to take part in the industrial boom.

New Goods

Typewriter, 1867
Barbed wire, 1874 (used for fences all over the United States)
Telephone, 1876
Phonograph (record player), 1877
Electric light, 1879
Gasoline automobile, 1885

Businesses hired hundreds of workers to do jobs in their factories. Cities became crowded, and low wages kept workers poor. Congress found the need to protect workers in the late nineteenth century. Workers began to form unions to fight the poor working conditions in the factories.

Many people moved to cities that had factories. These people included farmers, ranchers, and immigrants. They wanted to work in the factories. Large factories were hiring thousands of workers to control machines. Because more goods were being made, prices for goods were lowered. This meant that more people could afford goods. People bought the goods, which increased sales. With increased sales, a business could grow and grow.

3
Big Business

The growth of big business during the 1800s changed the American way of life. Cities became very crowded. Many workers did not make enough money to live comfortably. Many factory workers were very poor or poverty-stricken. Many children also worked in the factories. They did not go to school. This meant that they would never learn how to get away from a life of poverty. They would know only what it was to be a factory worker. Sometimes work slowed down if goods were not being bought. This caused some factories to close. People lost their jobs.

Immigrants and poor people moved into slums, or run-down areas, of town. Slums were unclean and dangerous. Many desperate people in the slums became thieves. People in slums did anything they could to survive. Most of these workers barely made extra money to enjoy life.

Some upper-level factory workers, such as managers, made enough money to afford houses.

Business owners did not live in slums. Many lived in mansions. They had a lot of money and power. They added to their wealth while the poor remained poor. During the late 1800s, many taxes were based on the things that a person owned. Many wealthy people hid what they owned from the government. They did this to avoid paying taxes.

Factory workers began asking for better working conditions. They wanted more pay, fewer work hours, and

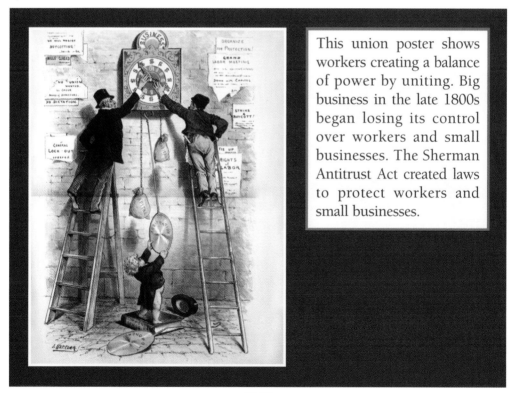

This union poster shows workers creating a balance of power by uniting. Big business in the late 1800s began losing its control over workers and small businesses. The Sherman Antitrust Act created laws to protect workers and small businesses.

safer factories. They asked local politicians or leaders to make new laws. The laws would stop factories and big business from abusing the workers. Unfortunately, many politicians were also businessmen. They were wealthy and powerful. Many politicians also had friends who were wealthy business owners. It was hard to get laws passed because many politicians favored big business.

Why Control a Market?

A business owner who had no competitors could ask for materials from suppliers at very low costs. The business owner would sell the finished goods at high prices to consumers.

For example, let's say a boot maker was able to get rid of his or her competition. The boot maker would go to the leather supplier. The leather supplier would have to sell leather for whatever the boot maker wanted to pay. Otherwise, the leather supplier would not make any money. The boot maker would finish the boots and charge high prices because he or she was the only boot maker left.

With little or no control by government, big business grew. Many business owners tried to get rid of competition. Some business owners tried to be the only company to offer a service or product in a town or city. This is called a monopoly. When a company has a monopoly, it has unfair and complete control over a product or service. Some big business owners bought smaller companies in order to get rid of them. Some small businesses joined to make one large corporation. A corporation is a group of companies that act as one company.

Some business owners united to form trusts. As a united group, business owners could control prices in a market. They could raise or lower prices. This would cause other businesses in the same market to fail. Trusts also set limits that could keep new businesses from forming or succeeding. These limits included licenses and patents. These were official papers that gave big business the only right to make certain goods or provide certain services. During the 1800s, there were many trusts. The tobacco, railroad, steel, and oil industries had trusts that ruled entire markets across America.

4

The Sherman Antitrust Act

Most Americans in the 1800s were not rich business owners. They were the workers of the middle and lower classes. During the mid-1800s, they began to unite. They asked political leaders for better living conditions. Most Americans wanted better schools, jobs, factories, and lives. They elected political leaders who were honest. They elected leaders who supported the issues of the working class.

Some state governments passed laws against trusts and monopolies. Trusts and monopolies were charged fines for trying to limit the success of other companies. The state laws were not perfect though. State laws could be enforced only within the state. Some companies could just move to another state where there were no laws against trusts. Also, state laws were not powerful enough to control large and national companies. National companies, such as railroad

National Control

The American people wanted national control of big business. They wanted a government that would work to protect the average American. This meant that government had to do at least three things:

- Maintain fair competition between businesses
- Protect the public interest or issues
- Relieve the poor and keep the wealthy honest

Laws needed to be tougher on the wealthy and big business. The government also needed to help the poor. It needed to provide better conditions for the working class. This could be done by controlling the trusts and monopolies of big business.

companies, did business in more than one state. Local laws did not apply to such large companies. National laws were needed to control national big business.

The United States Constitution gave Congress the right to control business dealings between the states and with foreign governments. Because of this, a law could be made

Senator John Sherman (1823–1900)

Senator John Sherman was born in Lancaster, Ohio. He began his career as a lawyer. He joined the Senate in 1861. The Senate is a branch of Congress. The Republican Party considered him for the United States presidency in 1880, 1884, and 1888, but he never ran for office. He retired from political life in 1898.

that would give Congress the right to control big business, monopolies, and trusts. Senator John Sherman set out to make this law.

Senator Sherman made a bill. A bill is the idea for a law. The bill is given to Congress. Congress decides if

The front page of the Sherman Antitrust Act (*at right*) shows that Congress had finally gotten serious about cleaning up big business. Senator John Sherman (*pictured above, in box*) was the first to see a need to help all people fight the power of the huge industries.

Congress of the United States of America;

At the First Session,

Begun and held at the City of Washington on Monday, the second day of December, one thousand eight hundred and eighty-nine.

AN ACT

To protect trade and commerce against unlawful restraints and monopolies.

Be it enacted by the Senate and House of Representatives of the United States of America in Congress assembled,

Sec. 1. Every contract, combination in the form of trust or otherwise, or conspiracy in restraint of trade or commerce among the several States, or with foreign nations, is hereby declared to be illegal. Every person who shall make any such contract or engage in any such combination or conspiracy, shall be deemed guilty of a misdemeanor, and, on conviction thereof, shall be punished by fine not exceeding five thousand dollars, or by imprisonment not exceeding one year, or by both said punishments, in the discretion of the court.

Sec. 2. Every person who shall monopolize, or attempt to monopolize, or combine or conspire with any other person or persons, to monopolize any part of the trade or commerce among the several States, or with foreign nations, shall be deemed guilty of a misdemeanor, and, on conviction thereof, shall be punished by fine not exceeding five thousand dollars, or by imprisonment not exceeding one year, or by both said punishments, in the discretion of the court.

Sec. 3. Every contract, combination in form of trust or otherwise, or conspiracy, in restraint of trade or commerce in any Territory of the United States or of the District of Columbia, or in restraint of trade or commerce between any such Territory and another, or between any such Territory or Territories and any State or States or the District of Columbia, or with foreign nations, or between the District of Columbia and any State or States or foreign nations, is hereby declared illegal. Every person who shall make any such contract or engage in any such combination or conspiracy, shall be deemed guilty of a misdemeanor, and, on conviction thereof, shall be punished by fine not exceeding five thousand dollars, or by imprisonment not exceeding one year, or by both said punishments, in the discretion of the court.

Sec. 4. The several circuit courts of the United States are hereby

21

a bill will become law. Senator Sherman gave the bill to Congress in 1890. Congress debated, or talked about, the bill. Some senators did not like the bill. They thought the Supreme Court would decide that the law was unconstitutional. This means that a law does not go along with the laws of the Constitution. The senators believed that the bill would not allow individual states to keep their own business laws. They also believed that Congress would never have the power to bring big business under control.

The bill was rewritten by the Committee of the Judiciary. This committee was in charge of making the bill more acceptable to Congress. The committee changed the first two sections of the bill. These sections made it clear that all business (in a state and between states) was under control of Congress. Congress accepted the new bill on April 20, 1890. It became an act, or law.

5

Protecting American Ways

The Sherman Antitrust Act made trusts illegal. Every activity to control a market was declared illegal. Any joining of companies for the purpose of controlling a market was also declared illegal. Any activities that seemed to limit fair competition were declared illegal. Any person found guilty of breaking the antitrust law would be fined up to $5,000. He or she might also be sentenced to a year in jail.

The act gave Congress and the federal government the power to bring charges against trusts. All trusts were to be dissolved. Charges would be fought in the Supreme Court. The Supreme Court would decide if the company was guilty of acting as a trust. For several years after the act was passed, trusts continued to form. The Supreme Court ruled in favor of some trusts. This kept the federal government from breaking up trusts.

Congress saw that it needed to strengthen the act. This would allow the federal government the power to control big business. Congress created more laws to support the act. It also formed new government agencies that would be on the lookout for trust activities. President Theodore Roosevelt campaigned against trusts in 1901. This brought more pressure on the Supreme Court to use the Sherman Antitrust Act against big business.

President Roosevelt became known as the Trust Buster. In 1903, he created a special agency, called the Bureau of Corporations. It was responsible for collecting information on businesses. If the agency found out that a company was violating the Sherman Antitrust Act, the government could bring charges against the company. During Roosevelt's presidency, the agency filed charges against more than forty companies. The most famous case happened in 1911.

In 1911, the Supreme Court ruled in favor of the federal government in the case against the Standard Oil Company. The Standard Oil Company was one of the most powerful companies in the world. There are companies today that came from this company. They include ExxonMobil and ChevronTexaco. John D. Rockefeller started the Standard Oil Company in Ohio in 1870. He soon bought most of the oil refineries throughout Ohio.

Theodore Roosevelt became known as the Trust Buster while president of the United States. He demanded that huge trusts be broken up to protect small businesses that wanted to produce goods for the same markets.

He built tankers to carry the oil. He also built pipelines that transported the oil through pipes. He formed businesses to advertise and sell his oil and goods. He bought up small companies to get rid of the competition.

In 1882, Rockefeller combined all of his companies into the Standard Oil Trust. It controlled more than 90 percent of the country's oil market. Small companies could not compete against this giant business. In 1892, an Ohio court ordered Standard Oil of Ohio to break away from the trust. Standard Oil of New Jersey took over the company's operations in 1899. It controlled thirty-seven smaller companies. Changing the state from Ohio to New Jersey allowed the companies to continue as a trust.

The U.S. Supreme Court ordered Standard Oil of New Jersey to dissolve in 1911. It decided that Standard Oil was violating the Sherman Antitrust Act. Thirty-three of the

The breakup of the Standard Oil trust happened in a Chicago, Illinois, courtroom in 1907. Judge Kenesaw Mountain Landis ruled that John D. Rockefeller's company was a trust. At the time, Standard Oil controlled more than 90 percent of the U.S. oil market.

smaller companies had to break away. They were not allowed to have any business contact with Standard Oil of New Jersey.

Congress created the Federal Trade Commission, or FTC, in 1914. The FTC was in charge of stopping any illegal business activities. In 1982, the FTC and government broke up the AT&T (American Telephone and Telegraph) Companies.

The Antitrust Division of the Department of Justice and the FTC watch big business even today. In 1998, the FTC and the Justice Department filed antitrust charges against the Microsoft Corporation. In 2001, Microsoft reached a settlement with the Department of Justice. Microsoft promised to protect fair competition and consumer freedom in the computer market.

Glossary

act (**AKT**)   A bill that has been passed by Congress. When signed by the president, it becomes law, or legal.

antitrust (**an-tee-TRUST**)   Against trusts, or groups of companies working together to get rid of competition or to control market prices.

consumer (**kun-SOO-mer**)   A person who buys and uses goods or services.

corporation (**kor-puh-RAY-shun**)   A group of people or companies that act as a single company.

economy (**ih-KAH-nuh-mee**)   The way a country or nation runs its industry, trade, and finance.

finance (**FYE-nans**)   The management and use of money by businesses, banks, and governments.

industry (**IN-dus-tree**)   Companies and businesses.

market (**MAR-kit**)   Products and services that can be bought and sold.

monopoly (**muh-NAH-puh-lee**)   A company, companies, or group that controls services or supply of a product.

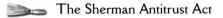

product (**PRAH-dukt**)   Something that is made
or manufactured.

regulate (**REH-gyoo-layt**)   To control or manage.

resource (**REE-sors**)   Something valuable or useful to a
place or person.

trust (**TRUST**)   A group of companies that work
together to get rid of competition or to control
market prices.

Web Sites

Due to the changing nature of Internet links, the Rosen Publishing Group, Inc., has developed an online list of Web sites related to the subject of this book. This site is updated regularly. Please use this link to access the list:

http://www.rosenlinks.com/aistc/shaa

Primary Source Image List

Page 5: 1894 *Harper's Weekly* illustration of business leaders parading in front of the U.S. Capitol. It is currently housed at the Library of Congress in Washington, D.C.

Page 8: Illustration of immigrants being interviewed for jobs at the Labor Exchange, New York City, in *Harper's Weekly,* 1868. It is currently housed at the Library of Congress in Washington, D.C.

Page 9: The United States Constitution, 1789. It is currently housed at the National Archives in Washington, D.C.

Page 11: Cover of the periodical *The Kentucky Farmer,* 1824. It is currently housed at the Filson Historical Society, Louisville, Kentucky.

Page 13: Nineteenth-century photo of a woodcut image of workers in a button factory.

Page 15: Photo of 1886 lithograph of labor gaining balance of power over business. It is currently housed at the Library of Congress in Washington, D.C.

Page 20: Photo of bust portrait of Senator John Sherman, circa 1860. It is currently housed at the Library of Congress in Washington, D.C.

Page 21: Front page of the Sherman Antitrust Act, 1890. It is currently housed at the National Archives and Records Administration, Washington, D.C.

Page 25: Photo of Theodore Roosevelt, twenty-sixth president of the United States, circa 1900.

Page 26: Photo of Judge Kenesaw Mountain Landis's courtroom, 1907. It is currently housed at the Library of Congress in Washington, D.C.

Index

About the Author

Holly Cefrey is a freelance writer. Her books have been placed on the Voice of Youth Advocates National Nonfiction Honor List. She is a member of the Authors Guild and the Society for Children's Book Writers and Illustrators.